GRIN - Verlag für akademische Texte

Der GRIN Verlag mit Sitz in München hat sich seit der Gründung im Jahr 1998 auf die
Veröffentlichung akademischer Texte spezialisiert.

Die Verlagswebseite www.grin.com ist für Studenten, Hochschullehrer und andere Akade-
miker die ideale Plattform, ihre Fachtexte, Studienarbeiten, Abschlussarbeiten oder Disser-
tationen einem breiten Publikum zu präsentieren.

D1742676

Dokument Nr. V129105 aus dem GRIN Verlagsprogramm

Susanne Grolle

CCTV to prevent crime?

To what extent does CCTV prevent crime and how does it effect the life in our cities?

GRIN Verlag

Bibliografische Information der Deutschen Nationalbibliothek: Die Deutsche Bibliothek
verzeichnet diese Publikation in der Deutschen Nationalbibliografie; detaillierte bibliografische Daten sind im Internet über http://dnb.d-nb.de/ abrufbar.

1. Auflage 2008
Copyright © 2008 GRIN Verlag
http://www.grin.com/
Druck und Bindung: Books on Demand GmbH, Norderstedt Germany
ISBN 978-3-640-35488-7

To what extent does CCTV prevent crime
and how does it effect the life in our cities?

To what extent does CCTV prevent crime and how does it effect the life in our cities?

Context

INTRODUCTION

The appearance of surveillance cameras in public areas in the UK (streets, parks, car parks, shopping malls etc) is obvious to everyone using these kinds of spaces. They are used to watch people's activities and behaviour and, if necessary react towards crime or anti-social behaviour.

The UK is by far the most advanced country in Europe in regards to public surveillance research and installation. In the last decade the coverage has grown dramatically. In 1990 there were three town centre schemes with approximately 100 cameras and in 2002 there were approximately 500 schemes with around 40,000 cameras.

The impression can be made that it is used as a general tool to prevent crime and promote a safer and cleaner community. But is it as effective as it promises to be and to what extent does it effect people's perception and activity in neighbourhoods and cities? To what extent does CCTV influences the urban designer work? What needs to be considered when implementing CCTV in existing and new developments?

This paper will help to understand the complexity of this question and issues related with its context.

One approach to the topic lays in the question: Why do people feel scared and insecure in public areas? The 'fear of crime' has become an important issue to consider within urban design and town planning. Being afraid of being a victim of crime can be positive if it leads to increased crime prevention, but it can also affect people's quality of life in a negative way. This fear gets projected on the appearance of places and their users which lead towards banning beggars and on-street traders. In the argument about public surveillance, it is often mentioned that constant camera monitoring is reducing this 'fear of crime'.

1. CCTV IN THE UK

1.1. What is CCTV?

Over the last decades Closed Circuit Television Cameras (CCTV) has become a crucial part of crime prevention and security schemes and is to be found in both private and public areas. Most of the time installed cameras are transferring the images to a control room where the scene is live-monitored by staff. There is the possibility for the staff to communicate with the police or to get in touch with local security personnel.

By the Home Office, CCTV is described as "a situational measure that enables a locale to be kept under surveillance remotely" (Gill, M., Spriggs, A. (2005) p. 1).

There are many different types of CCTV systems to apply to different requirements and to meet varying objectives. Cameras can be installed permanently, moved around a fixed point within an area or mobile when located in vehicles.

In some cases it might just be needed to review camera footage after a certain incident to help identify offenders and use of evidence.

The history of CCTV in the UK began in the 1980s when cameras were installed on the streets to identify activists during a strike of mine workers (1984). In 1985 football stadiums and Underground stations were beginning to install CCTV for surveillance. Three members of the IRA were sentenced to murder of two soldiers because of CCTV footage in 1990.

In 1998 a major CCTV initiative was set up under the Home Office Crime Reduction Programme which made £170 million available to fund a total of 684 CCTV projects. These projects have been completed and cameras are installed in a wide range of locations such as car parks, town and city centres, and residential areas.

Since 2007 a new type of CCTV has been trailed in different locations in the UK such as Middlesbrough. Cameras are connected to speakers which allow the workers in the control room to speak directly to the people. With this new method of direct response to behaviour a new era of surveillance has begun.

4

1.2. The theory behind CCTV

As its main aim CCTV is trying to reduce crime and discipline people's behaviour. Within this theory there are the following assumptions: [1]

- **Deterrence.** A potential offender is aware of the surveillance and assesses the benefits and risks of actions and chooses to either not offend or offend elsewhere
- **Efficient deployment.** Police assistance or security personnel can be called by the judgement of the staff monitoring the scene.
- **Self discipline.**
  By potential victim. Cameras act as a reminder of the risk of crime and behaviour gets changed accordingly.
  By potential offenders. The threat of potential surveillance produces self discipline[2].
- **Presence of capable guardian.** Based on the "Routine Activity Theory" [3] a crime needs a motivated offender, a suitable target and absence of a capable guardian. CCTV could act as such and may help reduce crime.
- **Detection.** Images of offences are taken by the cameras and may help to find, identify and punish offender.

The Illustration below shows that if a crime is to be committed, there needs to be a potential target or victim, an offender as well as an opportunity or absence of guardian. By removing one of these three factors, a crime can not be committed. There is a strong relationship between the environment, victim and offender, which has to be considered within the process of crime prevention.

Figure 1: The Crime equation.[4]

---

[1] Based on material of Armitage, R. (2002).
[2] Described as Bentham's Panopticon within Foucault, M. (1991).
[3] Cohen and Felson (1979)
[4] Source: British Waterways (2000).

5

2. EFFECTS OF CCTV

2.1. Effects on types of crime

There are a lot of studies and researches about the effect of CCTV on the different types of crime. For the purposes of this paper some will be summarized within the following.

Property crime
Property crime includes all offences towards the personal belongings of victims including vehicles, burglary, shoplifting, fraud etc.
Browns study of Newcastle upon Tyne, Birmingham and King's Lynn (1995) reveals that property crime was reduced in the CCTV covered areas. Although, thefts from vehicles and criminal damage increased, there was a reduction in theft of vehicles and shop offences. At the same time other significant measures such as traffic calming and pedestrianisation were introduced in the area which needs to be considered within the judgement of the effectiveness of CCTV by its own.
The Home Office published a study[5] with the following results:
- in five out of six car park evaluations there was a significant decrease in crime rates, overall reduction by 45%
- no significant effect on crime in public transport
- for city centres CCTV had a small but statistically significant reduction in crime of three per cent

The study summarises with the suggestion that CCTV has no effect on violent crime, a significant effect on vehicle crime and it is most effective when used in car parks.

Within sheltered housing schemes described and studied by Chatterton, M. & Frenz, S. (1994) CCTV proved to work efficiently in reducing burglary.

Personal crime
Personal crime includes drug-related offences, anti-social behaviour, abuse, violence, assaults etc.
There is evidence[6] that CCTV reduces assaults within smaller market towns but does not have less impact upon personal crime in larger metropolitan districts.
The study from Webb, B. & Laycock, G. (1992) about CCTV effectiveness within London Underground Stations showed that it reduced robberies but in stations that were smaller and less complex in their layout.

The CCTV systems with speakers have been showing a very high effectiveness as watching staff can respond to peoples' behaviour directly. This method creates a high awareness towards surveillance and is disciplining behaviour in public areas. That's the reason for its success against anti-social behaviour and littering offences in public areas

---

[5] Welsh, B. & Farrington, D. (2002).
[6] Brown, B. (1995).

within the studied area of Middlesbrough[7]. Because of the positive experience 20 communities throughout the country (e.g. Blackpool, Coventry, Northampton and the London boroughs of Southwark, Barking and Dagenham) have submitted proposals to create talking CCTV systems of their own, and have received funding from the Home Office.

2.2. Other effects

As well as effects directly on crime, CCTV can course effects such as displacement, fading and discrimination. These side effects will be explained in the following chapter.

A possible displacement of crime to surrounded areas is argued by Armitage, R. where crime is moved, not reduced.
Contrary, effects like diffusion of benefits which described the reduction of crime within surrounded areas are not covered by the CCTV scheme, is also occurring.
Most of the studied research[8] shows that the fear of crime was reduced. However, the methodology of its measure and the different fear of crime levels should be assessed and questioned.
As fear of crime is a very personal and subjective measure it is important to get professional questionnaires and representative answers to conclude the effects correctly.

The effectiveness of crime prevention schemes such as CCTV has to be watched and studied over a long period of time to be able to see its short and long term value. A possible fading of crime reduction after a certain time after the CCTV installation can be recognized. These time frames depend on the location and type of scheme are shown in the following some examples.

- Within London Underground Stations effectiveness of CCTV was reduced after approximately 12 months[9]
- Vehicular crime and criminal damage, effectiveness faded after approximately 8 months[10]

In general a fading of crime reduction could be prevented by maintaining the publicity of surveillance and its success. Interaction with the public and constant information flow as well as the obvious and common signs within the CCTV covered area could help towards constant crime prevention.
There is a controversial message from studies about the effectiveness of CCTV in regards to the deterrence of possible offenders. Offenders seem to take a blasé attitude when appearing in court and do not recognize CCTV as a serious problem. But when caught on camera, offenders are more likely to perceive CCTV as a risk which could then lead to a prevention of crime.

---

[7] Source: http://www.homeoffice.gov.uk/about-us/news/talking-cctv [15.03.2008].
[8] Chatterton, M. & Frenz, S. (1994), Brown, B. (1995), Mahalingham (1996), Sarno, C. (1996).
[9] Webb, B. & Laycock, G. (1992).
[10] Brown, B. (1995), Tilley, N. (1993).

.

Based on the fact that staff are watching the CCTV footage and action is taking place (contacting local security or police) on their personal judgement and training leads to criticism. Behind most CCTV scheme is a control room where people observe the images 24hours. These staff members need special training to fulfil their jobs as their judgement of the scene is vital to prevent crime. "Those monitoring CCTV have been found to adopt police categories of suspicion when viewing the screens." [11] This could lead to discrimination against certain groups of society (e.g. males, particularly black).

2.3. Data Protection Act 1998 & Human Rights Act 1998

CCTV systems have to be notified to the Information Commissioner (formerly data Protection Commissioner) under the Data Protection Act 1998. Along with this registration a number of legally enforceable principles are required. This means that collected information is gained fairly and lawfully as well as fulfils a certain code of practice such as:

- Signs in appropriate size (A3 or A4) must be display in CCTV areas, must show a 'purpose of the systems message'
- Data/images recorded should be used for original purpose planned for the scheme
- Cameras should be placed in locations where they avoid recording irrelevant or intrusive images
- Individuals have a right to a copy of any personal data captured only about them

Relevant part in the Human Rights Act 1998 state to following: [12]

- Everyone has the right to respect for his private and family life, his home and correspondence
- There shall be no interference by a public authority with the exercise of this right except such as in accordance with the law and is necessary in a democratic society in the interests of national security, public safety or economic well being of the country, for the prevention of disorder or crime, for the protection of health or morals, or for the protection of the rights or freedoms of others.

3. CCTV PROJECT IN KINGSTON UPON HULL

Kingston upon Hull announced in 1999 within the Crime and Disorder Strategy that a city-wide CCTV system of over 450 cameras will be deployed in and around the city until December 2000.
In 2004/2005 this system got extended to 520 cameras and is now one of the largest in the UK. The local authority, Kingston upon Hull City Council in partnership with Hull Community Safety Partnership allocated a total of £5 million towards the two-phased project.

---

[11] Armitage, R. (2002) p. 3.
[12] Armitage, R. (2002) p. 5.

The area covers most of the city centre, car parks, conservation areas and several listed buildings. Captured images are watched on 74 monitors in the control room located on the top floor at Festival House, Jameson Street. The CCTV system is directly linked to the Humberside Police Command Centre at Hessle. The CCTV operators are in radio contact with retailers, publicans and club owners through the Shop Watch, Pub Watch and Club Watch organizations. Operators also monitor the Councils intruder alarms and the Security Section provides a key holding service for all Council premises.

The impact and effectiveness of this scheme will be studied by the Dr. M. McCahill from the University of Hull. "The social impact of 'new surveillance' technologies: An ethnographic study of the 'surveilled'" will be the project title carried out from May 2008 until April 2010 and is funded by the ESRC.

The results of this study should be interesting considering that there are not a lot of studies about the people 'surveilled' and a need to understand the social impact of surveillance on people's lives.

4. CCTV AND URBAN DESIGN

In regards to Urban Design and Town planning CCTV and it's consideration with the design process has become more important over the last decades. Within city regeneration projects, private developments such as White City in West London and housing developments safety and security are important issues to inhabitants, users and landowners. Surveillance and crime prevention via CCTV is part of most of these projects.
The coordination with architects and planners during the design process is important to consider the appearance and maintenance of the CCTV equipment.
When implementing CCTV schemes within an existing development it often seems difficult to find the right location or type of system. But within a new development urban designers should use the possibilities of coordination and integration of CCTV systems.
To ensure a maximum benefit installed cameras in the correct location for surveillance and here they will need to be accessed, checked and maintained regularly. The integration of CCTV elements with street furniture should be aimed for to avoid street clutter and minimize the impact on the street appearance.
On the one hand CCTV cameras can be integrated into street lighting so that it is nearly invisible but on the other hand this method will have no or very little self discipline effect. The grade of CCTV integration needs to be carefully approached and considered.

A well processed network of communication between the staff watching the scene, local security and police force is crucial to the schemes' success.

5. DISCUSSION

To assess the effectiveness of CCTV as a single measure is a very difficult task as it is depending on other criteria such as location, population, police presence, traffic etc. It should always be used alongside other measures.

In case of CCTV there are a variety of discourses.
For instance, CCTV could be discussed through discourses on 'crime control', 'effectiveness' and 'community safety' or those stressing 'civil liberties', 'exclusion' or 'privacy'.
Questions like who owns the tapes rise and are very difficult to answer when most cameras monitoring public space are privately owned. Banks, office buildings, and department stores all routinely engage in continuous video monitoring of their facilities and of any adjacent public space. The recordings they make are privately owned, and may be stored, broadcast, or sold to other companies without permission, disclosure, or payment to the people involved. Video footage that is captured by public police departments may be considered part of the "public record," and as such are available for the asking to individuals, companies, and government agencies.
Critics[13] call CCTV "an instrument of social control and the production of discipline; the production of 'anticipatory conformity'; the certainty of rapid deployment to observed deviance and; the compilation of individualised dossiers of the monitored population".
How the media reflects and report these 'issues' is a crucial part within the judgement of how well CCTV is perceived from the public.
Reportage on CCTV has a little difficulty in reducing complex issues to common sense such as 'spy camera to catch vandals' (Evening Standard, 18 May 2001) or 'CCTV cuts crime on estate by 45%' (Daily Telegraph, 27 December 2000).
Current Reality TV shows such as "Street Crime UK" broadcast surveillance videos and police action which promotes positive reaction towards CCTV from the public.

By varies studies it has been proven that CCTV used in car parks, on motorways and against general vehicle crime is reducing crime and helps securing traffic and road safety.

The question of who profits the most by CCTV is very clear. As terror and organized crime becomes a major threat to the public, politicians need to react towards it. Surveillance with CCTV seems the only option and funding will be provided. The security industry increases and benefits from this process. Until 2003 there have been a total of 330 CCTV initiatives in the UK with an allocated budget from the Home Office of £105,778,536 million[14].

Apart from CCTV there are some options/additions to increase people's 'feel of security' and prevent crime. The layout and design of streets has to be easily read to insure street observation and viewing corridors. The design should avoid creating dark narrow

---

[13] www.appliedautonomy.com/isee/info.html [15.03.2008].
[14] Source: http://www.crimereduction.homeoffice.gov.uk/cctv/cctv21.htm [15.03.2008].

streets and the possibility to watch entrances and places of crowds of people. Pleasant and well maintained surroundings improve peoples' community sense and could therefore reduce crime. Following this idea, the concept of neighbourhood watch in combination with a good information flow can prevent crime as well.

6. CONCLUSION

Given heightened awareness of public safety and increased demand for greater security in the face of growing threats of terrorist violence, CCTV seems in most projects the ultimate solution. This work showed that the effects and benefits of camera surveillance are very different in each studied research so that a general statement towards the issue seems controversial. The information available seems very little and methodologically weak.

In general it can be said that camera observation in regards to vehicle crime (car parks, roads, motorways) is quite effective. Peoples' perception of CCTV is very different but in most cases people felt safer and less frightened to be a victim of crime. To maximize the benefit of CCTV schemes a regular maintenance check needs to be carried out as well as constant awareness and publicity campaign.

The bodies and companies who work with the tapes and their personal information should be aware of their responsibility towards to public. Therefore discriminatory while monitoring should be investigated and prevented.

It should never be supposed that CCTV will reduce crime regardless of considerations for the mechanisms under which it is expected to work or the local environment. In conjunction with other crime reduction measures such as traffic calming or increased police patrols, CCTV can be most beneficial when modified to local settings.

Overall it has to be stated that CCTV can be a useful tool to fight vehicle crime and to identify offenders but it will never be a single solution as crime has varies causes and patterns. Systems with connected speakers have been found to be very effective against anti-social behaviour and littering offences within public areas.

REFERENCES

Foucault, M. (1991) Discipline and Punish: The Birth of the Prison, Penguin.

McGuigan, J. (1996) Culture and Public Sphere: Routledge.

Madanipour, A. (2003) Public and Private Spaces of the City: Taylor and Francis Group.

Minton, A. (2006) The privatisation of public space: RICS Public Affairs, London.

Journals and Design Guidance

Brandon, G. (ed.) (2003) `National evaluation of CCTV: early findings on scheme implementation – effective practice guide´, Home Office Development and Practive Report, London.

British Waterways (2000) `Under Lock and Quay´, A Guide to Waterside Development and Improvement in London, Metropolitan Police & British Waterways.

Brown, B. (1995) `CCTV in town centres: Three case Studies´, Crime Detection and Prevention Series Paper 68, HMSO, Police Research Group, London.

Chatterton, M. & Frenz, S. (1994) `Closed Circuit Television: its Role in reducing Burglaries and the Fear of Crime in Sheltered Accommodation for the Elderly´, Security Journal, 5(3), pp. 133-139.

Cohen, L., Felson, M. (1979) `Social and Crime Rate Trends: A Routine Activity Approach´, American Sociological Review, 44, pp. 588-608.

Coleman, R. (2004) `Watching the Degenerate: Street Camera Surveillance and Urban Regernation´ Local Economy, 19(3), pp. 199-211.

Clark, P., Castell, B., Denham, K., Fowler, E. (2004) `Safer Places, The Planning System and Crime Prevention´, Office of the Deputy Prime Minister, Home Office, London.

Gerrard, G., Parkins, G., Cunningham, I., Jones, W., Hill, S., Dougls, S. (2007) `National CCTV Strategy´, Home Office, London.

Gill, M., Spriggs, A. (2005) `Assessing the impact of CCTV´, Home Office Research Study 292, London.

Mahalingham, V. (1996) `Sutton Town centre Public Perception Survey´ in Bulos, M. & Grant, D. (eds.) (1996) Towards a safer Sutton? CCTV One year on, London borough of Sutton.

Tilley, N. (1993) `Understanding Car parks, Crime and CCTV: Evaluation lessons from Safer Cities´, Crime Prevention Unit Series Paper 42, HMSO.

Webb, B. & Laycock, G. (1992) `Reducing Crime on the London Underground: an Elevation of Three Pilot Projects´, Crime Prevention Unit Paper 30, HMSO.

Welsh, B. & Farrington, D. (2002) `Crime prevention effects of closed circuit television: a systematic review´, Home Office Research Study 252, London.

Others

Armitage, R. (2002) To CCTV or not to CCTV, A review of current research into effectiveness of CCTV systems in reducing crime, Narco Crime and Social Policy Section, [Online], Available: http://epic.org/privacy/surveillance/spotlight/0505/nacro02.pdf [1.03.2008].

Griffiths, M. (2003) *Town Centre CCTV: An Examination of Crime Reduction in Gillingham, Kent*, [Online], Available: http://www.crimereduction.homeoffice.gov.uk/cctv/cctv33.pdf [1.03.2008].

Shepherd, J., Sivarajasingam, V. (2005) *Injury explains conflicting violence trends*, [Online], Available: http://injuryprevention.bmj.com/cgi/reprint/11/6/324.pdf [1.03.2008].

Krupa, F. (1993) *The Privatisation of Public Space*, [Online], Available: www.translucency.com/frede/pps.html [10.12.2008].

Lenger, F. (2006) *Die Zukunft der europäischen Stadt*, [Online], Available: http://hsozkult.geschichte.hu-berlin.de/forum/type=diskussionen&id=772 [6.01.2008].

http://www.crimereduction.homeoffice.gov.uk/cctv/cctv21yh.htm [15.03.2008].

http://www.crimereduction.homeoffice.gov.uk/cctv/cctv21.htm [15.03.2008].

http://www.homeoffice.gov.uk/about-us/news/talking-cctv [15.03.2008].

http://www.hull.ac.uk/socsci/research/projects/surveillance/index.html [15.03.2008].

CPSIA information can be obtained
at www.ICGtesting.com
Printed in the USA
LVIC041815300312

275511LV00003B